Janice VanCleave's
MICROSCOPES AND MAGNIFYING LENSES

JANICE VANCLEAVE'S
SPECTACULAR SCIENCE PROJECTS

Animals
Earthquakes
Gravity
Machines
Magnets
Microscopes and Magnifying Lenses
Molecules

JANICE VANCLEAVE'S
SCIENCE FOR EVERY KID SERIES

Astronomy for Every Kid
Biology for Every Kid
Chemistry for Every Kid
Earth Science for Every Kid
Geography for Every Kid
Math for Every Kid
Physics for Every Kid

Spectacular Science Projects

Janice VanCleave's
MICROSCOPES AND MAGNIFYING LENSES

*Mind-boggling Chemistry and Biology Experiments
You Can Turn Into Science Fair Projects*

John Wiley & Sons, Inc.
New York • Chichester • Brisbane • Toronto • Singapore

Design and Production by Navta Associates, Inc.
Illustrated by Doris Ettlinger

The publisher and the author have made every reasonable effort to insure that the experiments and activities in this book are safe when conducted as instructed but assume no responsibility for any damage caused or sustained while performing the experiments or activities in this book. Parents, guardians, and/or teachers should supervise young readers who undertake the experiments and activities in this book.

Library of Congress Cataloging-in-Publication Data
VanCleave, Janice Pratt.
  [Microscopes and magnifying lenses]
    Janice VanCleave's microscopes and magnifying lenses: mind-boggling chemistry and biology experiments you can turn into science fair projects.
    p.   cm. — (Spectacular Science Projects)
    Includes index.
    Summary: Includes directions for preparing science fair projects using microscopes or magnifying lenses in chemistry and biology experiments.
    ISBN 0-471-58956-X (acid-free paper)
    1. Microscopes—Experiments—Juvenile literature. 2. Magnifying glasses—Experiments—Juvenile literature 3. Microscopy—Experiments—Juvenile literature.
4. Biology—Experiments—Juvenile literature. 5. Chemistry—Experiments—Juvenile literature. 6. Science projects—Juvenile literature. [1. Science projects. 2. Microscopy—Experiments. 3. Biology—Experiments. 4. Chemistry—Experiments. 5. Experiments.]
I. Title. II. Title: Microscopes and magnifying lenses. III. Series: VanCleave, Janice Pratt. Janice VanCleave's spectacular science projects.
    QH278.V36   1993
    502'.8'2078—dc20   93-17352

Printed in the United States
10 9 8 7 5 4 3 2

CONTENTS

Dedicated to special friends who help me to see life more clearly,

Jean Biddle

Mary Lou Black

Beulah Bradford

Stella Cathey

Sue Dunham

Dianne Fleming

Weta Geib

Patsy Henderson

Kay Hogg

Dorothy Maynard

and

Ginger Russell

Introduction

Science is a search for answers. Science projects are good ways to learn more about science as you search for the answers to specific problems. This book will give you guidance and provide ideas, but you must do your part in the search by planning experiments, finding and recording information related to the problem, and organizing the data collected to find the answer to the problem. Sharing your findings by presenting your project at science fairs will be a rewarding experience if you have properly prepared for the exhibit. Trying to assemble a project overnight results in frustration, and you cheat yourself out of the fun of being a science detective. Solving a scientific mystery, like solving a detective mystery, requires planning and the careful collecting of facts. The following sections provide suggestions for how to get started on this scientific quest. Start the project with curiosity and a desire to learn something new.

SELECT A TOPIC

The 20 topics in this book suggest many possible problems to solve. Each topic has one "cookbook" experiment—follow the recipe and the result is guaranteed. The experiments are written so that you can perform the procedures even if you don't own a microscope. But in case you *do* have a microscope available, many experiments also include a special section called "Try It with a Microscope." Each "Try It with a Microscope" section provides an additional experi-

ment for you to perform once you have completed the original experiment. Approximate metric equivalents have been given after all English measurements. Try several or all of these easy experiments before choosing the topic you like best and want to know more about. Regardless of the problem you choose to solve, what you discover will make you more knowledgeable about microscopes and magnifying lenses.

KEEP A JOURNAL

Purchase a bound notebook in which you will write everything relating to the project. This is your journal. It will contain your original ideas as well as ideas you get from books or from people like teachers and scientists. It will include descriptions of your experiments as well as diagrams, photographs, and written observations of all your results. Every entry should be as neat as possible and dated. Information from this journal can be used to write a report of your project, and you will want to display the journal with your completed project. A neat, orderly journal provides a complete and accurate record of your project from start to finish. It is also proof of the time you spent sleuthing out the answers to the scientific mystery you undertook to solve.

LET'S EXPLORE

This section of each chapter follows each of 20 sample experiments and provides additional questions about the problem presented in the experiment. By making small changes to some part of the sample experiment, new results are achieved. Think about why these new results might have happened.

The experiments are written so that you can perform the procedures even if you don't own a microscope.

SHOW TIME!

You can use the format of the sample experiment to design your own experiments to solve the questions asked in "Let's Explore." Your own experiment should follow the sample experiment's format and include a single question about one idea, a list of necessary materials, a detailed step-by-step procedure, written results with diagrams, graphs, and charts if they seem helpful, and a conclusion answering and explaining the question. Include any information you found through research to clarify your answer. When you design your own experiments, make sure to get adult approval if supplies or procedures other than those given in this book are used.

If you want to make a science fair project, study the information listed here and after each sample experiment in the book to develop your ideas into a real science fair exhibit. Use the suggestions that best apply to the project topic that you have chosen. Keep in mind that while your display represents all the work that you have done, it must tell the story of the project in such a way that it attracts and holds the interest of the viewer. So keep it simple. Do not try to cram all of your information into one place. To have more space on the display and still exhibit all your work, keep some of the charts, graphs, pictures, and other materials in your journal instead of on the display board itself.

The actual size and shape of displays can be different, depending on the local science fair officials, so you will have to check the rules for your science fair. Most exhibits are allowed to be 48 inches (122 cm) wide, 30 inches (76 cm) deep, and 108 inches (274 cm) high. These are maximum measurements and your display may be smaller than this. A three-sided backboard (see drawing) is usually the best way to display your work. Wooden panels can be hinged together, but you can also use sturdy cardboard pieces taped together to form a very inexpensive but presentable exhibit.

A good title of six words or less with a maximum of 50 characters should be placed at the top of the center panel. The title should capture the theme of the project but should not be the same as the problem statement. For example, if the problem under question is *How can the size of small objects be compared?*, a good title of the project may be "Measuring with a Microscope." The title and other headings should be neat and large enough to be readable at a distance of about 3 feet (1 meter). You can glue

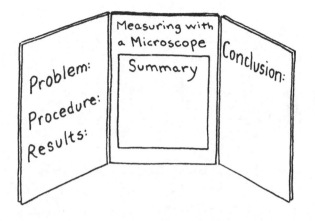

letters to the backboard (you can use precut letters that you buy or letters that you cut out of construction paper), or you can stencil the letters for all the titles. A short summary paragraph of about 100 words to explain the scientific principles involved is good and can be printed under the title. A person who has no knowledge of the topic should be able to easily understand the basic idea of the project just from reading the summary.

There are no set rules about the position of the information on the display. However, it all needs to be well organized, with the title and summary paragraph as the main point at the top of the center and the remaining material placed neatly from left to right under specific headings. Choices of headings will depend on how you wish to display the information. Separate headings for Problem, Procedure, Results, and Conclusion may be used.

The judges give points for how clearly you are able to discuss the project and explain its purpose, procedure, results, and conclusion. The display should be organized so that it explains everything, but your ability to discuss your project and answer the questions of the judges convinces them that you did the work and understand what you have done. Practice a speech in front of friends, and invite them to ask you questions. If you do not know the answer to a question, never guess or make up an answer or just say, "I do not know." Instead, you can say that you did not discover that answer during your research and then offer other information that you found of interest about the project. Be proud of the project and approach the judges with enthusiasm about your work.

CHECK IT OUT!

Read about your topic in many books and magazines. You are more likely to have a successful project if you are well informed about the topic. For the topics in this book, some tips are provided about specific places to look for information. Record in your journal all the information you find, and include for each source the author's name, the book title (or magazine name and article title), the numbers of the pages you read, the publisher's name, where it was published, and the year of publication.

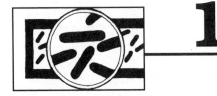

1

Water-Drop Lens

PROBLEM

Can you make a magnifier out of a water drop?

Materials

flat toothpick
petroleum jelly
sheet of newspaper
eyedropper
tap water

Procedure

1. Use the end of the toothpick to smear a thin layer of petroleum jelly over a word on the newspaper.

2. Fill the eyedropper with water, and squeeze one drop of water over one of the printed letters that have been covered with jelly.

3. Describe the shape of the water drop.

4. Look through the drop of water at the letter beneath it. Compare the size of the letter viewed through the water drop with the letters not covered by the drop.

Results

The water forms a round drop on top of the oily paper. The bottom of the water drop is flat, but the top is curved. The

letter under the water drop looks larger than the letters not underwater.

Why?

The paper under the water drop was covered with petroleum jelly to keep the water from soaking into the paper. Water and oil do not mix; thus, the water forms a dome on top of the oily surface. The rounded surface of the water drop acts like a **single convex lens** (a lens that is thicker in the center than on the ends; it curves outward on one side and is flat on the opposite side). A magnifying lens is made with a **double convex lens** (a lens thicker in the center than on the ends; it curves outward on both sides).

LET'S EXPLORE

1. Does the size of the drop affect its magnification? Repeat the original experiment using the toothpick to place smaller drops of water on the paper. Repeat again, using the eyedropper to add several drops to the same place on the paper, thereby forming one big drop. **Science Fair Hint:** Make diagrams to represent the size of the image viewed through the water drop. Next to the drawing, place the actual letter being viewed. Use these diagrams as part of a science project display.

2. Would the purity of the water affect the magnification of the drop? Repeat

SINGLE
CONVEX
LENS

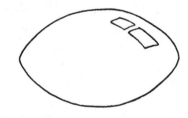

DOUBLE CONVEX
LENS

the original experiment using different samples of water, such as distilled water, bottled spring water, and tap water from different sources.

SHOW TIME!

1a. Make a hand-held magnifying lens by rolling a piece of clay into a long, thin rope. Use the clay to form a small circle in the center of a sheet of transparent plastic. Fill the center of the clay circle with water. Hold the plastic sheet over a sheet of newspaper and look through the water. Raise and lower the plastic sheet to get the best image.

b. Change the size of the clay circle and repeat the previous experiment. For each size circle, ask a helper to measure the distance from the lens to the newsprint that gives the best image. Photographs of the experiment with the distances labeled can be displayed.

CHECK IT OUT!

Light coming from an object is bent as it passes through a lens. Find out more about the bending or *refraction* of light rays. Where is the focal point of a lens? What is the focal distance?

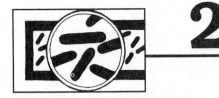
Larger and Smaller

PROBLEM

Can dense (having closely packed parts) material form lenses?

Materials

6-inch (15-cm) piece
    of 20-gauge wire
pencil
saucer
clear corn syrup

Procedure

1. Twist one end of the wire around the pencil to make a loop.

2. Remove the pencil from the loop.

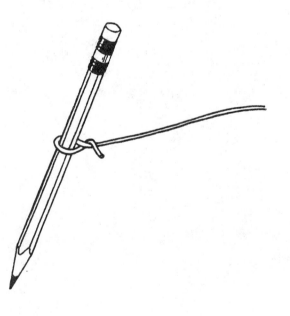

3. Fill the bottom of the saucer with corn syrup.

4. Bend the wire so that you can place the loop in the corn syrup. The loop should lay flat on the bottom of the saucer.

5. Carefully lift the loop out of the syrup. Make sure that a large drop of syrup remains in the hole of the wire loop.

6. Describe the shape of the syrup drop within the loop.

7. Hold the drop of syrup slightly above the point of the pencil.

8. Look down through the syrup drop and observe the pencil point. Raise or lower the loop to find a position that gives a clear image of the pencil.

9. Compare the size of the pencil point as it is viewed with and without the syrup-drop lens.

Results

Like a double-convex lens, the syrup drop is rounded on the top and bottom. The pencil point appears much larger when viewed through the syrup-drop lens.

Why?

Any dense material, such as clear corn syrup, can act like a magnifying lens—as long as the material is transparent and can form a shape with curved surfaces. The syrup molecules in the wire loop cling together, producing a curved surface above and below the loop. The top-and-bottom-curved surface produced by the syrup drop is called a double convex lens. This type of lens is found in microscopes and magnifying lenses. Objects can appear enlarged when viewed through a convex lens, whether the lens is made of glass or of clear syrup.

LET'S EXPLORE

1. Does the size of the syrup drop affect its ability to magnify? Repeat the original experiment twice: first make the loop larger in **circumference** (the distance around the outside of a circle), and then make the loop smaller in circumference.

2. How does the **viscosity** (the property that causes a liquid not to flow easily) of the liquid lens affect the magnification? Repeat the original experiment, replacing the thick syrup with solutions of syrup and water. Add varying amounts of water to the corn syrup to form samples of less viscous liquids. **Science Fair Hint:** Take and display photographs showing the procedure for making the wire lens holder.

Photographs taken during the experiments can also be displayed.

SHOW TIME!

Test the magnifying abilities of another dense material, such as gelatin. Ask an adult to prepare a gelatin mixture (lemon is more transparent than other flavors) using the directions on the box. Direct your adult helper to pour the gelatin into different-shaped containers, such as bowls or pans, to produce surfaces that are curved and flat. Each sample should be the same height. When cooled, remove each gelled sample from its container by dipping the outside of the container in warm water. Place the gelatin pieces on a section of newspaper, and observe the magnifying abilities of the different-shaped pieces.

3

Shape Up

PROBLEM

Does the shape of a lens affect its magnification?

Materials

clear plastic food wrap
clear drinking glass
tap water
sheet of newspaper

Procedure

1. Tear off a 12-inch (30-cm) piece of plastic wrap.

2. Line the inside of the glass with the wrap.

3. Pour about 2 inches (5 cm) of water into the lined glass.

4. Lay the sheet of newspaper on a table.

5. Set the glass of water on top of the newspaper.

6. Look down through the water and observe the newsprint.

7. Compare the size of the letters viewed through the water with the letters that are not covered by the glass of water.

8. Lift the plastic-wrap lining so that the bottom of the plastic is about 1 inch (2.5 cm) above the bottom of the glass. The bottom of the plastic wrap should now curve outward from the weight of the water.

9. Look through the curved water surface and observe the printed letters.

10. Describe any difference in the size of the letters viewed through the water with the letters that are not covered by the glass of water.

Results

When the surface of the water was curved, it **magnified** (caused to appear larger) the print; however, when the surface of the water was flat, there was no magnification.

Why?

The shape of the water's surface caused the magnification. When the surface of the water is curved outward, the water acts like a convex lens (a lens that is thicker in the center than at the edges;

it magnifies images of objects viewed through it). Light rays moving through the curved surface of the water lens are **refracted** (change direction). The bent light rays produce an enlarged image of the object.

LET'S EXPLORE

1. Does the depth of the water affect its magnification? Repeat the original experiment using different amounts of water in the glass.

2. How does the amount of curvature of the water's surface curvature affect the magnification? Repeat the original experiment using larger and smaller glasses. Vary the distance the plastic wrap is lifted from the bottom of the glasses to change the shape of the bottom of the plastic wrap.

SHOW TIME!

1a. Would a drop that curves inward affect the magnification? Build a lens holder by cutting a 2-inch × 4-inch (5-cm × 10-cm) piece of aluminum foil. Fold the foil in half lengthwise. Use the point of a pencil to poke a hole, about half the circumference of the pencil, in the center of the strip. Fold down 1 inch (2.5 cm) of each end of the strip to form support legs. Lay a sheet of newspaper on a desk near a lamp, and place the foil magnifier on top of the paper. Use an eyedropper to fill the hole in the foil with water. Look through the water lens and observe the size of the print. Very carefully touch the bottom of the water drop with the tip of your finger. You should remove only a very small amount of water from the drop, which will either drop to bulge outward, producing a convex lens, or to cave inward, forming a concave lens. Repeat this procedure until a concave lens is formed.

b. Repeat the previous experiment, this time making different-sized holes in the foil lens holder. Display the foil lens holder, along with diagrams of the images viewed through the different sizes and shapes of lenses.

CHECK IT OUT!

A lens is a curved, transparent object. Find out more about lenses. What is the difference between the shape of a convex lens and a concave lens? How do these lenses work? Do both lenses magnify? How does refraction of light by a lens cause magnification?

4

Magnifier

PROBLEM

What is the meaning of 2X magnification?

Materials

2-quart (2-liter) pitcher
tap water
round, clear, empty quart (liter) jar,
  with lid
baking pan
paper towel
sheet of lined notebook paper

Procedure

1. Fill the pitcher with water.

2. Place the empty quart (liter) jar in the pan.

3. Use the pitcher to fill the jar to overflowing with water. There should be no air bubbles left in the jar.

4. Secure the lid on the jar.

5. Dry the outside of the jar with the paper towel.

6. Place the jar on its side in the center of the notebook paper, with its lid pointing toward the side of the paper.

7. Slowly roll the jar toward you. Try to make the lines viewed though the bottle of water line up with the lines on the sheet of paper.

8. Describe the lines on the paper as viewed through the water.

9. Count the number of spaces on the sheet of paper that fit into one space between the lines as viewed through the jar.

Results

Looking through the jar of water makes the lines look farther apart. Two spaces on the sheet of paper used by the author fit into one space as viewed through the jar of water.

Why?

The distance between the lines as viewed through the jar of water is twice that of the distance between the lines on the paper outside the jar. This indicates that the **magnification** (the enlargement of an object's image) due to the water and glass of the jar is 2X. The expression *2X* means the image viewed through the magnifier is two times as large as the actual object.

A **compound microscope** is a microscope with two or more lenses. The lens closest to your eye is called the **eyepiece**, and the lens closest to the object being viewed is called the **objective lens**. The magnification of the eyepiece is usually 10X, and the microscope generally has several objective lenses of different magnification. The low-power objective lens of the author's microscope has a magnification of 10X, and the high-power objective is 60X. Combining the eyepiece and the low-power objective gives a magnification of 10 times 10, or 100X. The combination of the eyepiece and the high-power objective gives a magnification of 10 times 60, or 600X. The image of objects viewed through this compound microscope under low power looks 100 times as large as the object's actual size. The same object viewed through the high power appears to be 600 times as large.

LET'S EXPLORE

1. Does the shape of the jar affect its magnification? Repeat the original experiment using a jar with a larger circumference (the distance around the outside), such as a gallon (4-liter) fruit-juice jar or a plastic soda bottle. Repeat again using a jar with a smaller circumference, such as a tall, slender olive jar. **Science Fair Hint:** Glass containers are usually not allowed as

part of a project display. Experiment with as many plastic containers as possible and stand these in front of sheets of lined paper to demonstrate their magnifying abilities.

2. Would a greater magnification be achieved by filling the jar with a more viscous liquid? Repeat the original experiment, replacing the water with clear corn syrup or mineral oil.

SHOW TIME!

The area viewed through a microscope is called the **field of vision**. An increase in magnification changes the

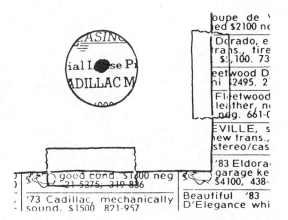

field of vision. Demonstrate this change by cutting a 1-inch (25-cm) hole in the center of two sheets of typing paper. The holes are to be equal in size. The holes represent fields of vision. Place one sheet of typing paper over a sheet of newspaper. Use the hole in the typing paper as a guide to draw a circle on the newspaper. Mark a dot in the center of the circle drawn on the newspaper.

Ask an adult to make an enlarged photocopy of the newspaper. Tape one of the sheets of typing paper over the enlarged copy and observe.

Tape the second sheet of typing paper over the original newspaper, and include both as part of a display.

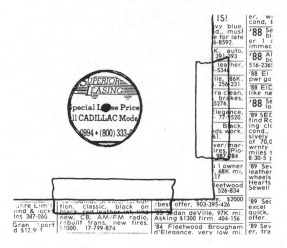

5

Doubles

PROBLEM

How do objects look through a compound microscope?

Materials

helper
sheet of newspaper with large print
masking tape (optional)
yardstick (meterstick)
2 magnifying lenses with a 3-inch
　(7.5-cm) diameter

Procedure

1. Have the helper hold up the sheet of newspaper so that it is at your eye level (or tape it to a door if you have no helper).

2. Stand about 1 yard (1 m) away from the newspaper.

3. Hold one magnifying lens in each hand.

4. Move the lens in your left hand in front of your left eye.

5. Close your right eye and look through the lens at the newspaper with your left eye.

6. Observe the letters as seen through the single lens.

7. Place the second lens directly in front the first lens.

8. Describe the letters as seen through two lenses.

9. Slowly move the second lens away from your eye and toward the newspaper until a clear image is seen.

10. Describe the image seen through the separated lenses.

11. Continue to look at the newspaper while your helper slowly moves the newspaper about 2 inches (5 cm) to the right.

12. Note the direction the paper appears to move when viewed through the lenses.

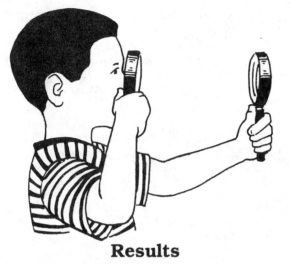

Results

When viewed through a single lens, the letters appear right side up, slightly enlarged, and very blurred. Through two lenses the letters are even more blurred, and moving the lenses farther apart produces sharp letters that are enlarged, upside down, and backwards. As seen through the lenses, the letters appear to move a greater distance and in the opposite direction.

Why?

The image seen through the two lenses is similar to images viewed through a compound microscope (a microscope with two or more lenses); both produce images that are enlarged, upside down, and backwards. The parts of a compound microscope can be compared to the lenses in this experiment. The lens closer to the eye acts like the microscope's eyepiece. The lens farther from the eye and closer to the object behaves similarly to the objective lens on a microscope. The distance between the two magnifying lenses in the experiment represents the length of the body tube on a microscope. Moving the lens back and forth is similar to turning the coarse-adjustment knob up and down on the microscope; both actions move the lenses a large distance away and toward the object being viewed.

LET'S EXPLORE

Does the distance of the lens from the object being viewed affect the image seen? Repeat the original experiment twice, first standing less than 1 yard (1 m) and then standing more than 1 yard (1 m) from the newspaper. Compare the sizes of the images seen at various distances and make note of any differences in the portion of the object seen. **Science Fair Hint:** Compare photographs taken during the experiment

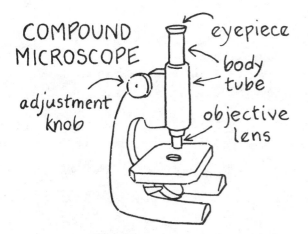

COMPOUND MICROSCOPE

eyepiece

body tube

adjustment knob

objective lens

with a drawing that identifies the parts and movements of a compound microscope.

SHOW TIME!

1a. Build and display a model of a compound microscope by wrapping a stiff piece of paper such as a file folder around the outside edge of a magnifying lens. Cut a slit in the paper for the handle of the lens. Secure the paper to the lens with masking tape, and then tape the sides of the paper together to form a tube. Cut a small window out of the bottom edge of the tube beneath the handle to allow light to enter. On the side opposite the handle, cut out a section that is just wide enough for the handle of a second magnifying lens to slip through and long enough for it to move up and down easily. Place the second lens inside the tube so that the lens handle sticks out. Stand the paper tube on the object being viewed. Hold the upper handle to keep the model steady as you move the lower lens up and down to **focus** (produce a sharp, clear image).

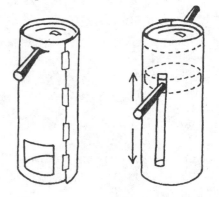

b. Repeat the previous experiment, this time forming tubes of different heights. Display photographs of the different models along with a description of their results.

6

Upside Down

PROBLEM

Why do images in a compound microscope appear upside down and backwards?

Materials

scissors
sheet of dark construction paper
flashlight
pencil
masking tape
square cardboard box, at least 12
  inches (30 cm) on a side
sheet of typing paper
magnifying lens
yardstick (meterstick)

Procedure

1. Cut a paper circle from the dark paper to fit over the lens of the flashlight.

2. Draw and cut the shape of half of an arrow from the center of the paper circle, as indicated in the diagram.

3. Tape the circle over the flashlight lens, as shown in the diagram.

4. Mark an X on a small piece of tape and place it on the rim of the flashlight to indicate the place to which the arrow on the paper circle is pointing.

5. Stand the cardboard box on a table, with its open side facing out.

6. Make a projection screen by taping the sheet of typing paper to the back inside wall of the box.

7. Turn the flashlight on and hold it against the typing paper with the X side up.

8. Slowly move the flashlight backwards toward you until an image of the arrow is seen on the typing paper.

9. Make a drawing of the arrow's image.

10. Hold the magnifying lens about 1 yard (1 m) from the typing paper.

11. Place the lens of the flashlight against the magnifying lens. Make sure the X side of the flashlight faces up.

12. Slowly move the flashlight back away from the lens until an image of the arrow is seen on the typing paper.

13. Make a drawing of the arrow's image.

Results

Without a magnifying lens, the image of the arrow pointed up and to the right.

With the lens, the image of the arrow pointed down and to the left.

Why?

Light travels in a straight line, but when it passes through the magnifying lens, it refracts (changes direction), causing the image to be upside down and backwards. Light passing through the objective lens of a microscope is refracted in the same manner as through the magnifying lens in this experiment. The bent light rays **converge** (come to a point) inside the tube of the microscope at a place called the **focal point**. The light continues to move in a straight line, forming within the tube an image that is smaller, upside down, and backwards. The person looking through the eyepiece, a convex lens at the top of the tube, sees the same image, but it is magnified. The final image formed by the eyepiece lens is reversed and much larger than the object being viewed.

LET'S EXPLORE

1. Does the distance of the lens from the screen affect the image produced? Repeat the original experiment, holding the magnifying lens at distances closer than 1 yard (1 m) from the screen.

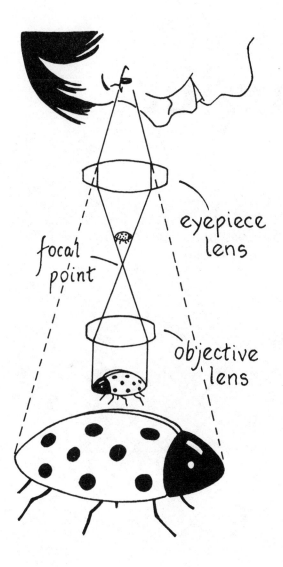

focal
point

eyepiece
lens

objective
lens

2. Does the size of the arrow design affect the image size? Repeat the original experiment twice: once placing a smaller arrow design over the lens of the flashlight, and once using a larger arrow design.

SHOW TIME!

Magnifying lenses and microscope lenses are convex. Use a single magnifying lens to demonstrate how an upside-down image is produced by darkening a room and holding the lens about 5 feet (1.5 m) from an open window. Ask a helper to stand in front of the window. Place a sheet of typing paper on the side of the lens opposite the window. Slowly move the paper toward and away from the lens until a small, focused, inverted image of your helper and the window forms on the paper. For more information about this experiment, see "Eye Lens," page 152 of *Biology for Every Kid* (New York: Wiley, 1990), by Janice VanCleave.

7

On Target

PROBLEM

How do the images of large objects fit on the retina of your eye?

Materials

pencil
2 sheets of graph paper
marking pen
gooseneck desk lamp
modeling clay
magnifying lens

Procedure

1. Lay the pencil in the center of a sheet of graph paper. Align the pencil with the lines on the paper.

2. Use the marking pen to trace around the edge of the pencil.

3. Count the number of squares that make up the length and width of the pencil tracing.

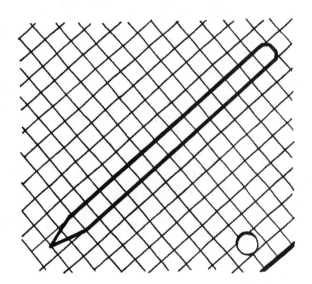

4. Turn the desk lamp so that its light shines to the side.

5. Darken the room except for the light from the desk lamp.

6. Use the small piece of clay to hold the pencil about 4 inches (10 cm) in front of the lamp.

7. Use the clay to hold the magnifying lens upright about 1 yard (1 m) in front of the lamp.

8. Hold a sheet of graph paper upright on the side of the lens opposite the lamp. The paper will act as a projection screen.

9. Slowly move the paper back and forth in front of the lens until a clear image of the pencil appears. Try to position the paper so that the image of the pencil is aligned with the lines on the paper.

10. Count the number of squares that make up the length and width of the image of the pencil.

Results

The image of the pencil produced by the magnifying lens is smaller than the actual size of the pencil. The reduction in the image size will depend on the strength of the lens. In the diagram, the lens reduced the image by one-fourth.

Why?

Inside each eye, just behind the **pupil** (the opening in the eye that shrinks or expands in response to light), is a small lens. Like the magnifying lens, the lenses in your eyes are called double convex because they curve outward on both sides. As light shines through a convex lens it is refracted (bent) inward. These bent rays meet at the focal point, and the distance that this point is from the lens is called the **focal length**. If the object, as in this experiment, is placed at more than two focal lengths beyond the lens, the image is inverted and smaller than the object. The lenses in your eyes produce a similar type of image, and therefore can fit onto your retina (the small area that acts like a projection screen on the back inside wall of your eye).

LET'S EXPLORE

1. How does the distance of the lens from the screen affect the image size? Repeat the original experiment twice, first by moving the screen to distances farther from the lens, and then by moving the screen to distances closer to the lens.

2. How does the distance of the lens from the object affect the image size?

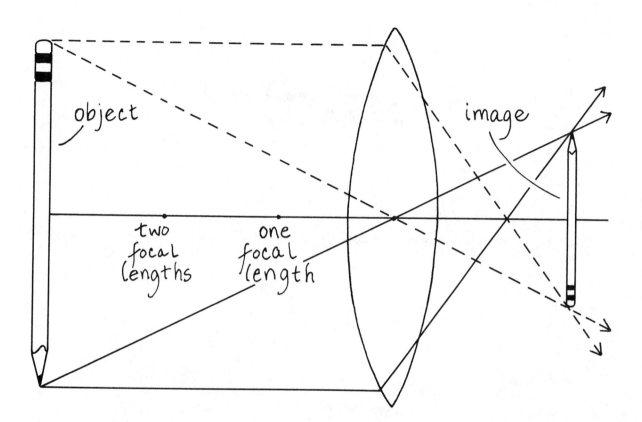

object

two
focal
lengths

one
focal
length

image

Repeat the original experiment again, moving the lens closer to the object.

SHOW TIME!

The kind of image formed by a convex lens depends on the distance of the ob-ject from the lens. Use a physical science text to find out how a convex lens can be used in microscopes to produce magnified images and in the eye to produce reduced images. Make diagrams representing the results of the different positions of the lens. Use these diagrams as part of a project display.

8

Spindles

PROBLEM

How can you observe the natural shape of Epsom salt crystals?

Materials

measuring cup (250 ml)
water
2 tablespoons (30 ml) Epsom salt
spoon
art brush
black construction paper
magnifying lens

Procedure

1. Fill the measuring cup one-fourth (63 ml) full with water.

2. Add the Epsom salt to the water.

3. Stir well. The solution will look cloudy and will have few undissolved salt crystals on the bottom of the cup.

4. Stir the water-Epsom salt solution with the bristles of the art brush.

5. Remove the brush, and paint a section of the letter J on the sheet of paper.

6. Stir the solution again with the bristles of the art brush.

7. Remove the brush, and paint another section of the letter on the paper.

8. Continue stirring the solution with the bristles of the brush and painting small sections of the letter, until the letter is completely formed.

9. Place the paper near a sunny window for several hours.

10. Use the magnifying lens to observe the letter on the paper every hour until the paper is completely dry.

Results

Results will vary depending on the humidity and the temperature of the air. It took three hours for the author's letter to dry on a day with low humidity and a temperature of about 68° Fahrenheit (20° C). At first, the edges of the letter dried, and tiny, shiny, clear crystals were seen. When completely dried, long spindles of clear, shiny crystals in starburst patterns formed the shape of the letter J.

Why?

Dissolving Epsom salt in water allows the molecules to separate and float freely through the water. As the water **evaporates** (changes from a liquid into a gas) from the solution, the Epsom salt molecules move closer together. The molecules all have the same shape, and they stack together like building blocks. As the water continues to evaporate, the salt molecules begin to stack in an orderly pattern, forming long, spindle-shaped crystals. The shape of the salt molecules determines the final shape of the crystals formed from the stacked molecules.

TRY IT WITH A MICROSCOPE

Microscope Procedure

1. Place a drop of water on a slide.

2. Dissolve one or two crystals of Epsom salt in the water.

3. Allow the slide to dry, and observe under low power. Move the slide around to view different areas.

Microscopic Results

Long, needle-shaped crystals form patterns that look like feathers.

LET'S EXPLORE

1. Do other crystalline solids have the same shape as Epsom salt? Repeat the original experiment, replacing the Epsom salt with table salt, alum, or sucrose (table sugar).

2. Are the microscopic structures of other crystals the same as those of Epsom salt? Repeat the microscope procedure, replacing the Epsom salt with table salt, alum, and sucrose.

Science Fair Hint: Make drawings of each observation, and display the drawings next to the crystals that were produced on the paper.

SHOW TIME!

Grow large salt crystals by pouring ½ cup (125 ml) of warm tap water into a quart (liter) jar. Add and stir table salt, 1 tablespoon (15 ml) at a time, until no more salt will dissolve in the water. Cut a 2-inch (5-cm) wide strip of black construction paper. The height of the paper should be about one-half the height of the jar. Stand the paper strip against the inside of the jar. Place the jar in a visible place where it will be undisturbed. Allow the jar to sit for three to four weeks. Using a magnifying lens, make daily observations of the area around the paper. Photographs taken of the day-to-day changes can be displayed.

CHECK IT OUT!

Crystals come in many sizes, shapes, and colors. Some, such as diamonds, are more valued than others, but they all have their own quality and beauty. Find out more about crystals. What is the definition of a crystal? Are all solids crystals?

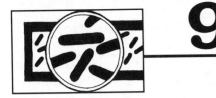

9

Poppers

PROBLEM

How do immiscible liquids (liquids that do not mix) behave?

Materials

baby-food jar with lid
tap water
red food coloring
spoon
clear liquid cooking oil
magnifying lens
desk lamp

Procedure

1. Fill the baby-food jar halfway with water.

2. Add one drop of red food coloring and stir.

3. Slowly add cooking oil to the jar until the jar is almost full.

4. Secure the lid and allow the jar to stand undisturbed for 2 minutes.

5. Describe the contents of the jar.

liquid oil

colored water

6. Shake the jar vigorously five times.

7. Close one eye and hold the magnifying lens near your open eye.

8. With your other hand, hold the jar in front of the lens with the light of the desk lamp behind the jar.

9. Study and describe the contents of the jar.

Results

At first, the entire contents of the jar have a pink color, but within seconds two separate layers begin to form: a red layer on the bottom, and a cloudy layer on top. Bubbles are seen rising and falling through the liquids. Many of the bubbles combine, forming larger bubbles.

Why?

The oil and water separate because they are immiscible. Shaking the jar produces an **emulsion** (a suspension of two liquids; some separate upon standing). Immediately after being shaken, bubbles of water and oil are seen throughout the mixture. When left standing, the lighter oil begins to float to the top and the colored water sinks to the bottom of the jar. The spheres of oil move toward each other because the molecules of oil attract each other. The attraction between molecules of the same material is called a **cohesive force**. This attraction causes smaller bubbles to be pulled apart, pop open, combine, and form larger bubbles. The spheres of water behave like the oil molecules by pulling on each other, causing small bubbles to combine and form

larger water bubbles. The two liquids finally separate into a layer of oil that floats on a layer of colored water.

TRY IT WITH A MICROSCOPE

Microscope Procedure

1. With an eyedropper, remove a sample from the jar containing the oil and water that has been vigorously shaken.

2. Squirt the liquid into the baby-food jar and then draw it back into the eyedropper. Repeat this action six or seven times to mix the liquid thoroughly.

3. Place a drop of the liquid on a microscope slide.

4. Observe under low power.

Microscopic Results

At first, the viewing field is dark and covered with tiny, moving bubbles. The bubbles appear to pop, and combine to form larger bubbles. As the bubbles grow larger and separate, the viewing field becomes lighter.

LET'S EXPLORE

1. How long does it take for the oil and water to completely separate? Repeat the original experiment. Ask a helper to start a timer as soon as you begin to shake the jar. At 10-minute intervals, use a magnifying lens to observe each layer, and record the time when no bubbles are observed.

2. Does the amount of shaking affect the time required for separation? Repeat the original experiment, but prepare two separate jars with equal amounts of oil and water in each. Shake one of the jars 5 times and shake the other jar 30 times. Allow both jars to sit undisturbed, and use a magnifying lens to determine when no bubbles are present in the separate layers.

SHOW TIME!

How can an emulsion be kept from separating? An emulsifying agent, such as an egg yolk, prevents an emulsion from separating. Prepare two mixtures as follows. One will contain an emulsifying agent, and one will not.

Mixture #1

In a large bowl, combine 1 tablespoon (15 ml) of water, 1 egg yolk, and 1 tablespoon (15 ml) of liquid cooking oil. Beat the mixture thoroughly then pour it into a clear jar and label it "WITH."

Mixture #2

Repeat the above procedure to combine 1 tablespoon (15 ml) of water and 1 tablespoon (15 ml) of liquid cooking oil Label the jar "WITHOUT."

Diagrams showing the contents of the jars after each action can be used as part of a project display.

Activator

PROBLEM

What effect does an enzyme have on a chemical reaction?

Materials

baby-food jar
3% hydrogen peroxide
adult helper
raw potato
magnifying lens

Procedure

1. Fill the baby-food jar halfway with 3% hydrogen peroxide.

2. Observe and record the contents of the jar for 2 to 3 minutes. Use diagrams as part of your description.

3. Ask the adult helper to cut a slice of raw potato that is large enough to stand upright in the jar.

4. Add the potato slice to the jar.

5. Use the magnifying lens to observe the surface of the potato that is beneath the liquid.

6. Continue to observe and record the contents of the jar every 5 minutes for a total of 30 minutes.

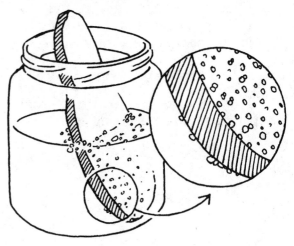

Results

The hydrogen peroxide in the jar looks like water; there are no visible changes. As soon as the potato touches the hydrogen peroxide, bubbles start collecting on the surface of the potato and rising to the surface of the liquid. At first, there is an increase in the bubbling around the potato. Foam starts collecting on the surface of the liquid; the amount of foam continues to increase, with larger bubbles seen throughout the frothy layer, until the bubbling decreases and finally stops.

Why?

Hydrogen peroxide **decomposes** (breaks apart) to form water and oxygen gas. This chemical change occurs when the liquid is sitting in an open container. Light also helps to make the breakdown occur. These are the reasons that hydrogen peroxide is stored in a tightly closed, dark bottle. The breakdown of hydrogen peroxide is so slow and the amount of oxygen gas released is so small that you are unable to detect it. Given enough time, bubbles would collect in the open container.

You can make the bubbles appear more quickly by adding a **catalyst** (a substance that changes the speed of a chemical reaction, but is not changed itself).

Catalysts found in living cells are called **enzymes**. Enzymes speed up the breakdown of complex food chemicals into smaller, simpler, more usable parts. The enzyme from the potato causes the hydrogen peroxide to break apart quickly into water and oxygen gas. The oxygen gas is responsible for the foam collected on the surface of the liquid.

TRY IT WITH A MICROSCOPE

Microscope Procedure

1. Ask your adult helper to cut a potato in half.

2. Scrape the edge of a clean microscope slide across the cut surface of the potato several times, until a white liquid collects on the slide.

3. Use a toothpick to transfer the liquid to the center of a clean microscope slide.

4. Cover the liquid with a coverslip.

5. While observing under low power, ask your helper to add one drop of hydrogen peroxide to the edge of the coverslip.

Microscope Results

The liquid from the potato appears to be a collection of different-shaped transparent and **opaque** (cannot be seen through) objects. Dark bubbles appear at the instant the hydrogen peroxide is added and continue to grow until they cover the entire viewing field.

LET'S EXPLORE

Do all plant cells contain the same amount of catalyst chemicals? Repeat the original experiment using slices of fruits and vegetables such as apples, pears, celery, and carrots. Compare the speed of bubble production in the hydrogen peroxide and the amount of foam produced. **Science Fair Hint:** Diagrams of the results, along with photographs or magazine pictures of the fruits and vegetables used, can be included as part of a project display.

SHOW TIME!

1a. Many laundry detergents contain enzymes. Enzymes are added to detergents to break apart protein molecules that stain clothing. Test for the presence of enzymes in a detergent sample by pouring ¼ cup (63 ml) of hydrogen peroxide into a clear plastic glass. Add ½ teaspoon (2.5 ml) of detergent with enzymes. Use a magnifying lens to observe the contents of the glass.

b. Repeat the previous experiment using different detergents with and without enzymes. Use the speed of the evolution of bubbles to compare the amount of enzyme in each detergent. Prepare a chart listing the detergents used and their results. Photographs can be used to demonstrate the experiment.

CHECK IT OUT!

Hydrogen peroxide is used to clean wounds. The frothing that occurs when the liquid is poured into a wound is the result of the breakdown of the hydrogen peroxide by the enzymes found in the cells of your body. Use a biology text to find out more about enzymes. What role do enzymes play in human digestion?

11

Spotted

PROBLEM

How is water transported through plants?

Materials

2 drinking glasses
tap water
red food coloring
celery bunch with leaves
adult helper
paper towels
magnifying lens

Procedure

1. Fill each glass one-fourth full with water.

2. In one glass, add enough red food coloring to turn the water bright red.

3. Select two stalks from the innermost part of the celery bunch. They should have leaves and a pale green color.

4. Ask an adult helper to cut across the bottom of each celery stalk.

5. Stand the cut end of one celery stalk in the glass of red water, and the other in the clear water.

red water   clear water

6. Leave the celery stalks in the glasses overnight.

7. Remove the stalks of celery from the glasses, and dry each stalk with a paper towel.

8. Use the magnifying lens to study the entire outer surface of each celery stalk.

9. Ask your adult helper to cut a 2-inch (5-cm) section from the bottom of each stalk.

10. Use the magnifying lens to study the cut surfaces of each section.

11. Ask your adult helper to cut a 2-inch (5-cm) section from each stalk at the end nearest the leaves.

12. Again, use the magnifying lens to study the cut surfaces of the celery sections.

Results

The leaves and stalk of the celery standing in the clear water are green. The stalk taken from the red water has reddish-colored leaves, and tiny red stripes can be seen running down its entire length beneath the surface. Sections cut from both stalks have a single row of tiny dots near one outer edge. These dots are red in the section cut from the stalk that was in the red water. The surfaces of the cross sections cut at the top and bottom of the same stalk are similar.

Why?

The cross sections of the celery stalk revealed that the colored water rose from the bottom of the stalk through tiny tubelike structures to the top of the stalk. These water-carrying vessels in plants are called **xylem** tubes. The red food coloring stains the thick walls of the xylem tubes, so they appear as red circles on the cross sections. In nature, xylem tubes transport a liquid mixture of water, sugars, and minerals up to the leaves of the plant. This watery mixture is called **sap**.

TRY IT WITH A MICROSCOPE

Microscope Procedure

1. Ask your adult helper to cut a very thin slice from each stalk of celery.

2. Place the slices on separate microscope slides.

3. Observe and make a drawing of each slide as seen through the microscope.

Microscope Results

Small, colorless cells crowd together around the outer edge of the celery slices, surrounding larger cells, which are side by side in the center. Large, dark-looking masses appear near one edge of each slice and are red on one of the slices.

LET'S EXPLORE

Do flower stems contain xylem tubes? Repeat the original experiment using a white carnation. **Science Fair Hint:**

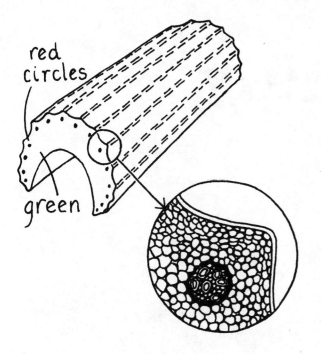

red circles

green

Make colored diagrams of the results of the experiment and use them as part of a project display.

SHOW TIME!

Are xylem tubes connected to each other? With the help of an adult, cut the stem of a white carnation lengthwise about halfway up the stem. Carefully separate the two halves, placing one in a glass of blue-colored water and the other in a glass of red-colored water. Observe the color of the flower after 48 hours. Study slices of the flower's stem under a microscope or magnifying lens. Photographs of the flower petals before and after the experiment can be used as part of a project display.

12

Bumpy

PROBLEM

How do bacteria help some plants live?

Materials

trowel
clover plants
quart (liter) plastic bucket
tap water
paper towels
magnifying lens

Procedure

1. Use the trowel to dig up a clover plant. Be sure to get as much of the root as possible.

2. Fill the bucket about halfway with water.

3. Dip the roots of the clover plant up and down in the bucket of water until the roots are free of dirt.

4. Lay the wet plant on a paper towel. Blot the plant with another paper towel to absorb any excess water.

5. Close one eye and look through the magnifying lens.

6. Move the plant back and forth in front of the magnifying lens until it is clearly visible. Slowly turn your body in different directions until the best light source is found.

7. Study the roots of the plant carefully. Find the nodules (rounded bumps) growing on the roots.

Results

Small nodules that look like tiny potatoes seem to be growing on the roots. Some of the nodules are separate and appear at different places along the roots; however, most of the nodules are grouped together in clumps at the top of the roots.

Why?

In order to live, plants need the nitrogen compounds that are found in soil. Nitrogen gas makes up 78 per cent of the earth's atmosphere, but plants cannot use this form of nitrogen. Bacteria called **nitrogen-fixing bacteria** change nitrogen gas into nitrogen compounds that plants can use. Some nitrogen-fixing bacteria live in the soil, while others live on the roots of plants such as clover. The

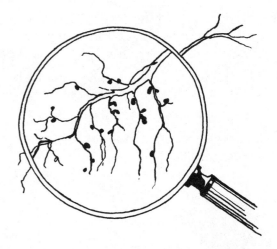

bacteria enter the root hairs of the plant, and as they multiply a nodule forms. The bacteria and clover help each other. The bacteria "fix" nitrogen gas so that the plant can use it, and the plant provides food for the bacteria. This is an example of **symbiosis**: when two organisms, living together, are mutually benefited.

TRY IT WITH A MICROSCOPE

Microscope Procedure

1. Use scissors to cut a section about ½-inch (1.3-cm) long from one of the smaller roots. The piece must contain at least one small nodule.

2. Place the root section on a microscope slide.

3. Position a desk lamp so that the slide is brightly lit from above.

4. Adjust the mirror under the stage of the microscope to produce a dark background for the viewing field.

5. Slowly move the slide around while viewing it under low power.

Microscope Results

The outside surface of the nodules looks rough and bumpy, while the root has a smoother appearance.

LET'S EXPLORE

1a. Are the nodules hollow? Ask an adult to cut a nodule in half. Use a magnifying lens to examine the content of the nodule.

b. Place the open nodule on a microscope slide and examine it using the previous microscope procedure. **Science Fair Hint:** Photographs of the clover nodules, along with diagrams of images viewed through the microscope, can be used as part of a project display.

SHOW TIME!

People are simply imitating nature when they recycle resources. Elements that are important to life, such as nitrogen, are naturally recycled. Nitrogen is found in the air, in soil, and in all living things. Use a biology text to find a diagram of the nitrogen cycle. Prepare a display chart of the nitrogen cycle. Photograph plants and animals needed for the chart, and use the photographs on the chart instead of drawings.

 **13**

Floaters

PROBLEM

How does a penicillium mold grow and what does it look like?

Materials

baby-food jar
dishwashing liquid
warm tap water
apple cider
magnifying lens

Procedure

WARNING: After performing the experiments in this chapter, discard all molds and the foods on which they are grown. SKIP THIS ENTIRE CHAPTER IF YOU ARE ALLERGIC TO MOLD.

1. Wash the jar with warm, soapy water and rinse with warm tap water.

2. Fill the jar with apple cider.

3. Place the open jar of apple cider in a warm, dark place.

4. Use the magnifying lens to study the surface of the apple cider in the jar; make daily observations of the surface of the cider for two weeks.

Results

After a few days the surface of the cider appears to have round, fuzzy blue-green floating pads on it. These circles resemble floating lily pads. In time, the growths cover the entire surface of the liquid.

Why?

The powdery growth on the surface of the apple cider is the mold **penicillium**. The time it takes for penicillium mold to grow depends on the temperature of the room. In a warm room, signs of growth may appear in two to three days. This blue-green mold is one of the most common and widespread of all fungi. The base of the floating penicillium pad is made up of threads called **hypha**. This tangled mass of hypha is called a **mycelium**. At the top of each hypha thread is a blue green spore. The large number of spores gives penicillium its bluish-green

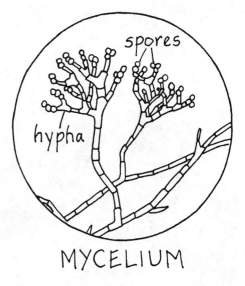

MYCELIUM

color and fuzzy appearance. Besides its medicinal purposes, penicillium is used to make cheeses such as Roquefort. This cheese is blue because of the large numbers of spores present.

TRY IT WITH A MICROSCOPE

Microscope Procedure

1. Collect a sample of the mold by gently brushing an art brush across the surface of the mold.

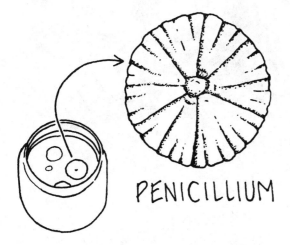

PENICILLIUM

2. Tap the brush on a clean microscope slide.

3. Observe the slide under low power.

4. Adjust the mirror below the slide to produce as much illumination as possible.

5. Move the slide around to view different areas.

Microscope Results

Dark clumps and specks as well as threadlike structures are seen across the viewing field.

LET'S EXPLORE

1. Would the penicillium mold grow in a closed jar? Repeat the original experiment, placing a lid on the jar.

2. Does the type of fruit juice affect the results? Repeat the original experiment using other fruit juices such as cranberry, grape, and cherry.

SHOW TIME!

1a. Will mold grow on solid foods? Place a slice of bread in a sealable plastic bag. Add ten drops of water to the inside of the bag. Seal the bag and place it in a dark, warm place for ten days. Use a magnifying lens to observe the surface of the bread daily for signs of mold. Make colored diagrams of your observations.

b. At the end of ten days, ask an adult to cut a thin slice from the bread piece. Place the slice on a microscope slide. Slowly move the slide around as you observe it under low power, with the slide brightly lit from above by a desk lamp. Make a colored diagram, and display with diagrams of the bread mold observed with the magnifying lens.

CHECK IT OUT!

The penicillium mold is used to make the antibiotic called *penicillin*. Find out more about the penicillium mold. What is an antibiotic? How did the British scientist Sir Alexander Fleming discover that penicillium mold had antibiotic properties?

14

Baby Plant

PROBLEM

What does the inside of a seed look like?

Materials

10 pinto beans
baby-food jar
tap water
refrigerator
spoon
paper towels
magnifying lens

Procedure

1. Place the beans in the baby-food jar.

2. Fill the jar with water.

3. Place the jar in the refrigerator overnight.

4. Use the spoon to remove the beans from the jar.

5. Place the beans on a paper towel to absorb the excess water.

6. Use your fingernail to carefully remove the outer covering from one of the beans.

7. Use your thumbnail to pry the round end of the bean open. Separate the two halves of the bean very gently so as not to break the inner parts. If the inner parts of the bean are broken, repeat steps 6 and 7 with another bean.

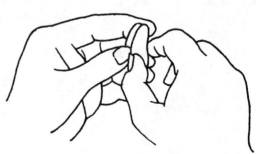

8. Lay the two halves of the bean on a clean paper towel, with the inside of each bean half facing up.

9. Use the magnifying lens to study the structure of each bean half.

10. Use the diagram on the next page to find each of these parts on your bean: *cotyledon*; *epicotyl*; *hypocotyl*; *radicle*.

Results

What appears to be a baby bean plant is found inside the bean.

Why?

Within every seed are basic structures that will develop into a plant. The function of each of these structures is described on the next page.

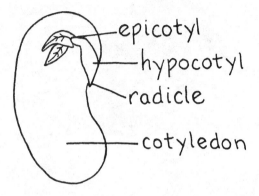

- **Epicotyl**—The first true leaves of the plant.

- **Hypocotyl**—This structure will develop into a stem.

- **Radicle**—Develops into the main root of the plant.

- **Cotyledon**—Stores food for the young plant until it can make its own food. A bean is a dicotyledon, commonly called a **dicot**, because it has two cotyledons.

In many plants, when a seed is first formed it is not ready for planting. It must first go through a **dormancy period** (time of inactivity). The seed does not grow during its dormancy period, but it *does* change chemically in order to prepare the baby plant inside for further development. After these chemical changes occur, the seed is ready to be planted—whereby **germination** (the beginning of growth or development) of the baby plant takes place within the seed. Germination can occur only if there is a proper amount of oxygen, water, and a suitable temperature. Each type of seed requires its own amount of oxygen, water, and warmth.

LET'S EXPLORE

1. Do other dicots have baby plants inside? Repeat the experiment, replacing the pinto beans with comparably shaped beans such as lima beans.

2. Do **monocots** (seeds with one cotyledon) have baby plants inside? Repeat the original experiment, replacing the pinto beans with corn kernels, a common example of a monocot. Adult assistance may be needed to open a corn kernel.

SHOW TIME!

Flowering plants are called angiosperms and are classified into two groups called dicots and monocots. Prepare a

ANGIOSPERMS			
Group	Leaf Structure	Flower Parts	Xylem and Phloem Bundles in Stem
monocot	parallel veins	three or multiples of three petals	scattered throughout
dicot	branched veins	four or five, or multiples of four or five petals	in a ring

chart showing the differences between the two groups. Use the data chart above to aid you in finding examples of dicot leaves and flowers. Photograph the leaves and plants of each seed group and display the photographs on your chart. Use the microscope procedure below to study the location of the xylem and **phloem** (food-carrying) transport tubes in the stems of each group.

TRY IT WITH A MICROSCOPE

Microscope Procedure

1. Ask an adult to cut thin cross sections from the stems of a dicot and a monocot.

2. Place the sections of stems on separate slides.

3. Observe the stem sections under low power.

4. Move the slides around to locate the thick-looking bundles of cells making up the transport tubes.

Microscope Results

In the cross sections of each stem, the bundles of xylem and phloem tubes are seen as dark circles. In the dicot, all the circles are arranged in a ring around the stem. In the monocot, however, the circles are scattered randomly throughout the stem.

15

Identity

PROBLEM

How are fingerprints transferred and analyzed?

Materials

transparent tape
desk lamp
magnifying lens

Procedure

1. Tear off about 1 inch (2.5 cm) of transparent tape and stick it across the tip of your index finger.

2. Remove the tape from your finger.

3. Hold the tape so that the light of the lamp shines through the tape.

4. Examine the tape by looking at it through the magnifying lens.

5. Identify the pattern formed by your fingerprint by comparing it with the three basic fingerprint patterns: whorl, loop, and arch.

BASIC FINGERPRINT PATTERNS

whorl loop arch

Results

A copy of your fingerprint is left on the sticky side of the tape.

Why?

Your body has two layers of skin. The outer skin is called the **epidermis**, and the deeper second layer of skin is called the **dermis**. The boundary between the dermis and the epidermis is not straight and smooth; it consists of small folds. These folds produce a series of ridges and grooves in areas where the skin is thick: the palm of the hand, sole of the foot, and fingertip, for example. The patterns formed by the ridges on the fingertips are called **fingerprints**. There are three basic fingerprint patterns—whorl, loop, and arch—but no two people have been found with exactly the same fingerprints. Beneath the surface of the epidermis are oil-producing glands. A thin layer of oil from these glands collects on the fingertips. When the tips of your fingers touch anything, a little oil in the form of a fingerprint is left.

TRY IT WITH A MICROSCOPE

Microscope Procedure

1. Place a piece of transparent tape on a microscope slide and observe the tape under low power. This will make you familiar with the magnified surface of the tape so that you will not mistake it for part of your fingerprint.

2. Rub the sharpened end of a pencil across a sheet of paper 15 to 20 times to collect a layer of graphite on the paper.

3. Rub your index finger across the graphite on the paper.

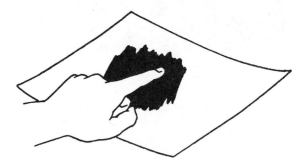

4. Tear off about 1 inch (2.5 cm) of tape and stick it across the graphite on your finger.

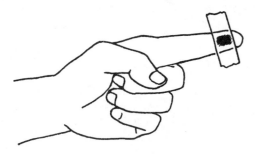

5. Remove the tape and stick it to a second, clean microscope slide.

6. Slowly move the slide around as you observe it under low power.

Microscope Results

The surface pattern of the tape can be seen beneath the wide rows of black clumps of graphite. A single row of graphite covers most of the viewing field. The rows are not in straight lines, but curve.

LET'S EXPLORE

1. Do each of your fingers have the same fingerprint pattern? Repeat the original experiment, examining the prints from each fingertip. **Science Fair Hint:** Make an outline of each hand on separate sheets of typing paper. Rub the fingerprint of each of your fingers in powdered paint. Collect the colored fingerprints with clear tape as before. Place each piece of tape on the corresponding finger in the hand diagrams. Identify the pattern for each fingerprint taken. Use the diagrams as part of a science fair display.

2. How do fingerprints of the same basic pattern differ? Use a magnifying lens to compare the prints from two people with the same basic fingerprint pattern. Determine the differences in the prints.

SHOW TIME!

Does everyone in the same family have the same basic fingerprint pattern? Prepare print samples from the index finger of each family member. Ask each person to press his or her finger against an ink pad and then against a sheet of typing paper. Label the print with the person's name and relation to you. Prepare a poster with the prints, and use them as part of a project display.

16

Expander

PROBLEM

What happens to a latex sponge in water?

Materials

latex dishwashing sponge
magnifying lens
tap water
saucer
scissors
ruler

Procedure

1. Stand the dry latex sponge on its long edge. If necessary, hold it upright.

2. Observe the upturned side of the sponge with the magnifying lens.

3. Describe the appearance of the sponge as viewed through the magnifying lens. Make a diagram to represent your description.

4. Pour enough water into the saucer to cover its bottom.

5. Cut a ½-inch (1.3-cm) square section from the dry sponge.

6. Stand the small sponge section in the water.

7. With your unaided eye, observe any change in the size of the sponge.

8. Use the magnifying lens to observe the surface of the sponge.

Results

The surface of the dry sponge has holes that vary in size and shape. The color of the sponge is not significant because color is added by the manufacturer. Adding water causes the surface of the sponge to expand slightly in all directions. After the addition of water, the sponge, as viewed through a magnifying lens, looks wet and shiny, with holes that are slightly larger than when the sponge was dry.

Why?

Sap from rubber trees is called **latex**. Chemicals are added to this liquid sap, and the mixture is then whipped into a foam. The foam is poured into molds, heated until dry, cooled, and then removed from the molds. It is now a soft material with air spaces throughout. This spongy, water-absorbing material is used to clean everything from dishes, cars, and dogs to your body. This factory-made sponge behaves very much like a natural sponge in its ability to absorb water. Both the factory-made sponge and the natural sponge have open spaces that allow water to move from one cavity to the next. As the water fills each space, the sponge expands.

TRY IT WITH A MICROSCOPE

Microscope Procedure

1. Use scissors to cut a thin slice from the dry sponge.

2. Use your fingers to stretch the sponge slice as much as possible, then place the slice onto a microscope slide.

3. Under low power, observe the sponge. Use a dissecting probe or straightened paper clip to move the slice around until the best view of the holes of the sponge is located.

4. Hold the sponge against the slide with the probe. At the same time, place drops of water next to one side of the sponge using an eyedropper.

Microscope Results

The dry sponge appears as a dark object with irregular-shaped holes. The holes close when the water is added.

LET'S EXPLORE

1. Are all liquids absorbed by a dry sponge? Repeat the original experiment using different liquids such as syrup, mineral oil, and rubbing alcohol. *WARNING: Keep rubbing alcohol away from your mouth and nose.*

2. Does a natural sponge behave in the same manner as a latex sponge? Repeat the original experiment using a natural sponge.

SHOW TIME!

Living sponges are very unusual animals found in aquatic (watery) environments. The thin layer of flattened, protective cells covering the surface of a sponge is punctured with tiny holes. Water is able to move through the openings in both the real and the factory-made sponges. Use different samples of factory-made and living sponges. Cut equal-sized pieces from each sample. Compare the amount of water that each will hold by submerging each piece in a bowl of water and squeezing the water into a measuring cup. Display the samples with the experimental results.

17

Modified

PROBLEM

What are the different parts of a finger-nail?

Materials

soap
tap water
paper towel
magnifying lens

Procedure

1. Wash your hands with soap and water.

2. Dry your hands with the paper towel.

3. Use the magnifying lens to examine your fingernails.

4. Use the diagram to identify the parts of your nails.

5. Use the magnifying lens to study the skin around the nails.

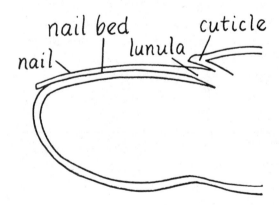

Results

The part of the nail that covers the finger is pink; the nail looks white where it extends past the end of the finger. There is often a whitish, half-moon-shaped area near the base of the nail. Some nails have white spots. The skin around the nail often looks dry and scaly.

Why?

Your fingernails are simply made up of skin cells that have been pressed together tightly to form a thin, rigid plate. The **nail bed** is the pink, fleshy area beneath the nail that provides a smooth surface for the growing nail to glide across, and its pink color is caused by the rich supply of blood beneath it. All the growth of a nail takes place beneath the whitish, half-moon-shaped area known as the **lunula**. The ridges and bumps on a nail are due to uneven growth of the nail at its **root** (the area beneath the lunula). White, irregular-shaped flecks in the nail are bubbles of air trapped between the cell layers. The **cuticle** is dead skin around the base and sides of the fingernails.

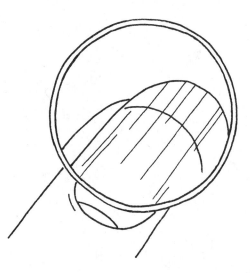

TRY IT WITH A MICROSCOPE

Microscope Procedure

1. If you do not have a nail that extends past the end of your finger, find a helper who does.

2. Place the finger with the longest nail on the stage of the microscope.

3. Position a desk lamp so that the nail is brightly lit from above.

4. Under low power, study the structure of the top surface or the tip of the nail.

5. Paint the end of the nail with a thin layer of red fingernail polish.

6. Again, observe the nail tip under low power.

Microscope Results

The nail's surface varies from one individual to the next, but no one's nails are smooth. The red polish aids in observing the variations or roughness in the nail's surface.

LET'S EXPLORE

Do toenails look the same as fingernails? Repeat the original experiment, observing toenails instead of fingernails. Since it is difficult to observe your own toenails, use the toenails of a helper. **Science Fair Hint:** Make diagrams of your nails as viewed with your unaided eye and as viewed through the magnifying lens and microscope. Describe the nails and label the structural parts. Use the diagrams as part of a project display.

SHOW TIME!

Like fingernails, hair is made up of modified skin cells. A color pigment called **melanin** in the hair shaft determines the actual color of the hair. Find out why some hair turns gray or white. Collect samples of hair from a person who has both natural-colored and gray hair. Observe the hair samples with a magnifying lens or a microscope. Display the samples in a sealed plastic bag with diagrams of their magnified appearance, along with an explanation of the differences in color.

CHECK IT OUT!

Temperature seems to affect the growth rate of nails; nails grow faster in the summer months than during the winter. Nails on the longest finger grow faster; those on the shortest fingers, more slowly. Use a science encyclopedia to find out more about fingernails. What is the average rate of growth for nails? Do nails on the right hand grow at a different rate than those on the left hand? Do toenails grow at the same rate as fingernails?

18

Jerky

PROBLEM

How are water fleas collected and what do they look like?

Materials

adult helper
wire clothes hanger
scissors
knee-high stocking
sewing needle
sewing thread
baby-food jar with lid
rubber band
paper towel
magnifying lens

Procedure

1. Ask your adult helper to bend the hanger to form a 4-inch (10-cm) loop at one end, as shown in the diagram.

2. Use the scissors to cut the toe out of the stocking.

3. Open the cut end of the stocking and place the wire loop inside.

4. Fold the top of the stocking over the edge of the wire loop, and stitch around the fold with the needle and thread to secure the stocking to the wire.

5. Stretch the other end of the stocking over the mouth of the baby-food jar and secure it with the rubber band.

6. Have your adult helper select a place along the bank of a pond. Choose a spot with some plant growth in the water along the shore.

7. Place the jar and wire loop into the water.

8. While holding the end of the wire, move the loop toward plants growing in the water. The jar will be pulled through the water.

9. When the jar is full of water, allow excess water to drain out of the stocking before moving away from the pond.

10.. Remove the rubber band and lift the stocking off the jar.

11. Place the lid on the jar and dry the outside of the jar with the paper towel.

12. Close one eye and hold the magnifying lens near your open eye.

13. With the other hand, hold the jar in front of the lens.

14. Move the jar back and forth in order to see its contents clearly. Slowly turn your body in different directions to find the best light source.

15. Study the contents of the jar and look for a tiny organism that moves through the water with a jerky movement. If you do not see this organism, collect another sample. *NOTE: Return the water and contents of the jar to the pond. Wash* *your hands after working with pond water.*

Results

Every sample will produce slightly different results. Varying types of plant and animal life can be collected; thus, the descriptions will vary from sample to sample and from pond to pond.

Why?

One common pond creature is **daphnia**, an organism about ¹⁄₁₀ inch (.25 cm) long that is visible with the naked eye and moves with a jerk. Daphnia are often called "water fleas" because they appear to jump through the water. The feathered antennae of the daphnia serve as oars, and propel the organism through the water in a series of jerky movements.

TRY IT WITH A MICROSCOPE

Microscope Procedure

1. Place a few strands pulled from a cotton ball in the center of the slide.

2. Observe the contents of the jar of pond water in order to find an organism that is visible to the naked eye.

3. Insert an eyedropper into the water, placing the tip as close to the organism as possible.

4. Draw the organism, along with some water, into the eyedropper.

5. Hold the eyedropper upright, allowing the organism to sink to the tip of the eyedropper.

6. Squirt a drop of the material onto the cotton strands and place a coverslip on the drop (see Appendix #2 for more detailed instructions on making this slide).

7. Move the slide around slowly, observing the specimens under low power. For the best view, reduce the light on the slide.

Microscope Results

The cotton strand and coverslip help to limit the movement of the water organisms, making it easier to observe their structure.

LET'S EXPLORE

Do all ponds contain the same water organisms? Repeat the original experiment, collecting speciments from different ponds. You might take your collecting net on vacation too. **Science Fair Hint:** Take photographs of the ponds and display them with diagrams of the organisms viewed in the water samples.

SHOW TIME!

Are different organisms seen at different depths in the pond? Use the collecting net and jar to collect samples from the surface and the bottom of the water along the bank. Prepare microscope slides from each water sample. Make sure you include any debris. Study the slide under low power, moving it around to observe all areas. Prepare diagrams of the organisms found in each sample, and use Appendix #3 as well as biology texts to identify the organisms.

 **19**

Break Away

PROBLEM

How are coins affected by routine handling?

Materials

sheet of typing
desk lamp
5 used pennies
5 new pennies
magnifying lens

Procedure

1. Place the sheet of typing paper on a table under the lamplight or near a window.

2. Place 5 used pennies and 5 new pennies on the paper so that the image of the Lincoln Memorial faces up.

3. Use the magnifying lens to observe any differences in the image on the used and new coins.

4. With your unaided eye, look at the center of the Lincoln Memorial on each coin.

5. Now use a magnifying lens to look at the center of the Lincoln Memorial on each coin, and note any difference.

Results

The image on the new pennies is sharper and easier to see. The image on the used pennies looks smoother, and on some coins small details are not visible. All the coins have a raised area, but it is difficult to identify the object with the unaided eye. With a magnifying lens, you can see a sharp image of Abraham Lincoln sitting inside the building. The same image of the man is visible on the used coins, but is much less clear.

Why?

The image on each coin is changed by a process called **erosion**. Erosion is the loosening and eventual wearing away of particles that make up an object. Every time a coin is touched, small particles of metal on its surface are moved slightly. After enough handling, metal pieces break away. In time, the surface of each coin becomes smooth. This same process occurs on rocks, buildings, statues, and other objects that are touched by wind, water, or human hands.

TRY IT WITH A MICROSCOPE

Microscope Procedure

1. Lay one of the pennies on a microscope slide.

2. Position the desk lamp so that the coin is brightly lit from above.

3. Under the low-power objective of a microscope, study the surface of the coin, Lincoln Memorial side up.

4. Move the coin around to observe its surface.

5. Study the surfaces of several used and new coins.

Microscope Results

Specks of dirt and corrosion not visible with the naked eye or magnifying lens can be observed on the coins. **Science Fair Hint:** Drawings of the microscopic views can be made and displayed to represent the degree of erosion on used and new coins.

LET'S EXPLORE

Does the metal on all coins erode from handling? Pennies are made of copper. Repeat the original experiment using coins made of different metals, such as nickel. If possible, observe coins from different countries. **Science Fair Hint:** A collection of the different coins used in the experiment can be used as part of a project display.

SHOW TIME!

How do chemicals affect metallic surfaces? Show the effect of acid on coins made from copper by placing a folded paper towel in a saucer. Pour enough vinegar into the saucer to wet the towel and place five or more new pennies on top. After 24 hours, observe the surface of the coins as in previous experiments with a magnifying lens and a microscope. Check with a chemistry teacher for information about the chemical reaction between vinegar and copper that produced the green coating, or see "Green Pennies," page 92 in *Chemistry For Every Kid*, (New York: Wiley, 1989), by Janice VanCleave. Before-and-after photographs taken of the coins, along with diagrams and descriptions of the observations, can be displayed.

Grainy

PROBLEM

What kinds of particles make up soil?

Materials

sheet of paper
1 teaspoon (5 ml) of dry soil (a sample
   can be collected from outside or
   from an indoor flower pot)
magnifying lens

Procedure

1. Place the sheet of typing paper on a
table near a window with direct sun-
light.

2. Spread about ½ teaspoon (2.5 ml) of
soil onto the paper.

3. Observe the soil through the magnifying lens. Note the differences in the
shapes, sizes, and colors of the soil
particles. Determine which type of particle is most abundant in the sample.

4. Rub the soil between your thumb and fingers. Observe how the soil feels as you rub it between your fingers.

5. Allow the particles to fall onto the paper.

6. Study the soil again through the magnifying lens.

Results

The description will vary depending on the type of soil. Generally the sample will contain small twigs; tiny, irregularly shaped stones (usually brown or grey); small, irregularly shaped, clear glassy pieces; tiny balls; and specks of brown dirt. The texture or feel of the soil changes as you rub it between your thumb and finger. At first, it feels smooth, but it changes to a grainier texture. The twigs, stones, and glassy pieces are surrounded by tiny specks of brown dirt.

Why?

The texture of the soil changes after being rubbed because the smooth dirt balls break up and fall away, leaving the hard stones and sand grains behind. Soil contains particles of various sizes, which determine the texture of the soil. The largest particles are stones and gravel; these are irregularly shaped pieces of rock and are larger than .08 inch (.2 cm) in diameter. The next smallest-sized particles are sand grains; these particles look like pieces of clear, rounded glass and are smaller than .08 inch (.2 cm).

Some of the particles have diameters less than .00016 inch (.0004 cm) and would require a powerful microscope in order to be seen. The amount of each kind of particle in a soil sample not only determines the name given to the soil, but how it behaves. An example is soil that is called sandy. Sandy soil contains at least 70 percent sand and does not hold water well because there are large spaces between the grains. Sandy soil is loose, allowing water to drain through rapidly.

TRY IT WITH A MICROSCOPE

Microscope Procedure

1. Rub a soil sample between your thumb and finger, allowing the particles to fall onto a microscope slide.

2. Place a coverslip over the particles and press gently to flatten them.

3. Position the desk lamp so that the slide is brightly lit from above, and use the mirror or light attachment on the microscope to project light onto the slide from below.

4. Move the slide around to study all areas.

Microscope Results

Some of the particles look transparent and others are **opaque** (materials that light does not pass through). The sizes and shapes of the particles vary.

LET'S EXPLORE

Repeat the original experiment using samples of a soil collected from different locations. Samples taken from house plants may contain small, round pieces of white plastic foam. **Science Fair Hint:** Collect soil samples from different locations while on a vacation or ask friends and relatives to mail you some. Use information learned about the different samples, their location, and their appearance under a magnifying lens and/or a microscope as part of a project display.

SHOW TIME!

Use an earth science text to discover more about soil horizons, and the differences in soil color, texture, and composition in each layer. Collect samples of soil at different depths and study their appearances with magnifying instruments. Look for a place where a road has been cut into a hill or mountain, because this provides a good cutaway section of different soil horizons. Photographs of this roadside area, along with drawings of magnified views of the soil samples, can be displayed.

Appendix 1

THE COMPOUND MICROSCOPE

Microscopes may vary in appearance and complexity, but basically they have the same parts. Carefully study the labeled parts of the compound microscope in the diagram. The numbers 10X and 40X on the objective lenses mean that these lenses magnify the size of the object 10 and 40 times. The eyepiece is also marked 10X. This makes the combined magnification under low power 10×10, or 100 times. The magnification under high power is 10×40, or 400 times. The function of each labeled part is as follows:

- **Eyepiece**—Contains a lens.

- **Body Tube**—Aligns the eyepiece and objective lenses above the viewing field.

- **Revolving Nosepiece**—Holds the objective lenses, and turns to place one lens at a time beneath the body tube.

- **Objective Lenses**—Low-power and high-power lenses of different magnifications.

- **Stage**—Platform where specimens are placed.

- **Stage Clip**—Holds specimens on the stage.

- **Diaphragm**—Adjusts the size of an opening to vary the light that is reflected into the viewing field.

- **Mirror or Lamp**—Directs light through the diaphragm and onto the specimen on the stage.

- **Coarse Adjustment**—Each turn of the wheel raises and lowers the body tube in large increments from the stage.

- **Fine Adjustment**—Each turn of the wheel raises and lowers the body tube in small increments from the stage.

- **Arm and Base**—Body of the microscope.

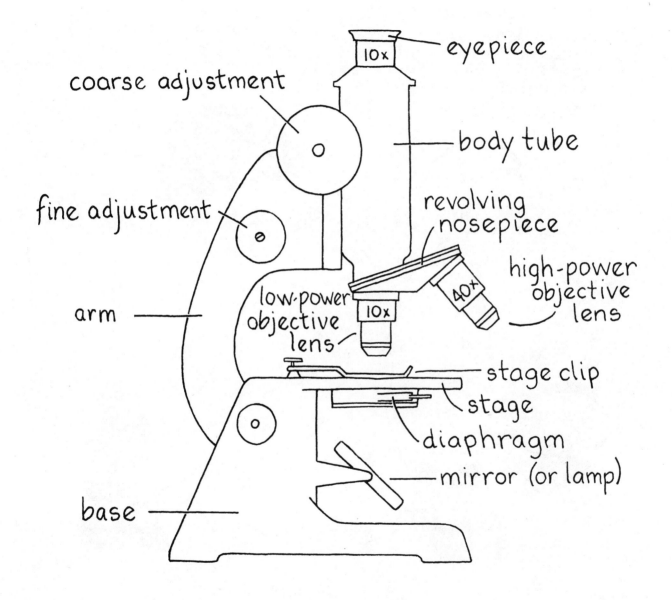

eyepiece

10x

coarse adjustment

body tube

fine adjustment

revolving nosepiece

high-power objective lens

40x

arm

low-power objective lens

10x

stage clip

stage

diaphragm

mirror (or lamp)

base

USING THE MICROSCOPE

1. When moving the microscope, carry it upright with both hands. Hold the microscope by placing one hand on its arm and the other hand under its base.

2. Set the microscope away from the edge of the table and keep it in this position.

3. Begin each observation by making sure the lowest-power lens is under the body tube. Turn on the microscope light if one is available, or adjust the mirror under the stage to reflect light up through the hole in the stage. You should see a bright circle of light when looking through the eyepiece.

4. Place a slide on the stage by raising the body tube with the coarse adjustment. The low-power objective should be about 1 inch (2.5 cm) above the stage. Slip the slide with the specimen you want to observe under the stage clips and above the center of the hole in the stage.

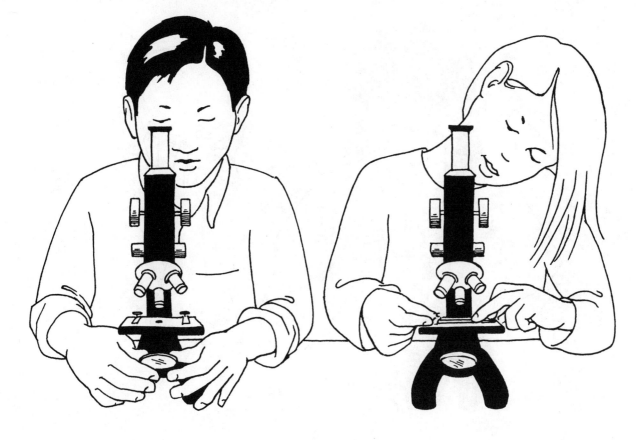

5. Use the coarse adjustment to lower the body tube to a position just above the slide. Look through the eyepiece. Slowly raise the body tube using the coarse adjustment until the specimen comes into view. If you turn too quickly and pass it, repeat this step slowly. If you move the body tube back toward the stage, you might break the slide. You may focus downward with the coarse objective if at its lowest position the lens rests above the slide. Use the fine adjustment to bring the specimen into sharper focus. Move the slide around slowly to observe all of the specimen. Adjust the light until you see the specimen as clearly as possible.

6. To change to a higher magnification, first find the specimen with the low-power lens. Then, without moving the body tube, rotate the next-higher-power lens under the body tube. The specimen should be in view and only adjustments made with the fine adjustment are needed to bring it into focus. If the specimen does not come into view simply by rotating the lens, slowly move the slide around in order to position the specimen under the lens. Adjust the light or mirror to provide more or less light. Thin specimens work best.

7. When looking at thick specimens, place a desk lamp so that its light shines down directly onto the top surface of the specimen, and observe under low power.

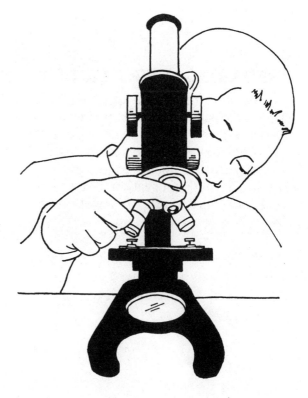

Appendix 2

PREPARING A WET MOUNT

A **wet mount** is a slide specimen that has been prepared with a drop of water and covered with a small piece of glass. This is done to keep some specimens from **dehydrating** (losing water) and shrinking during observation. Use the following procedure to prepare a wet mount.

1. Lay a clean slide on a table.

2. Place the specimen in the center of the slide.

3. Use an eyedropper to place one drop of water in the center of the specimen.

4. Hold the coverslip (a small, square piece of glass) so that one side just touches the edge of the drop of water. Let the coverslip drop. A few bubbles under the coverslip will not interfere with observing the specimen, but you may need to make a new slide if too many bubbles are trapped.

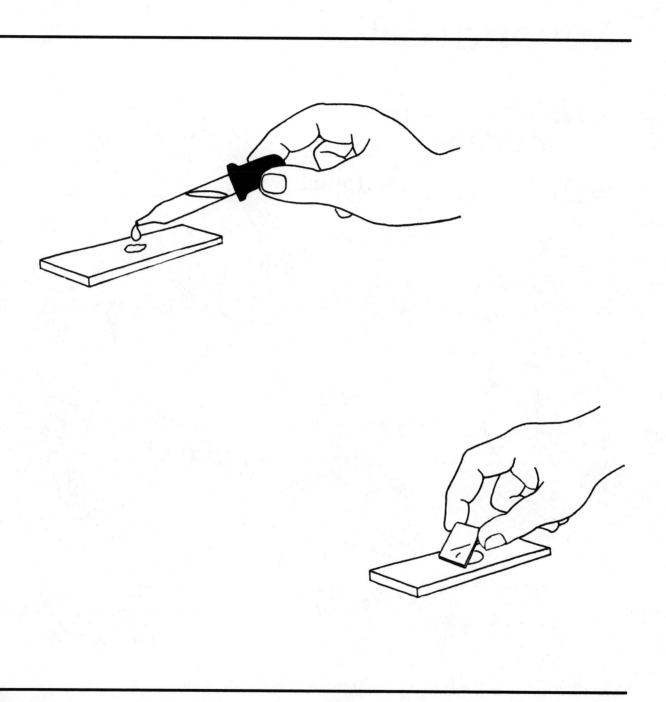

Appendix 3

COMMON POND-WATER ORGANISMS

ANIMALS

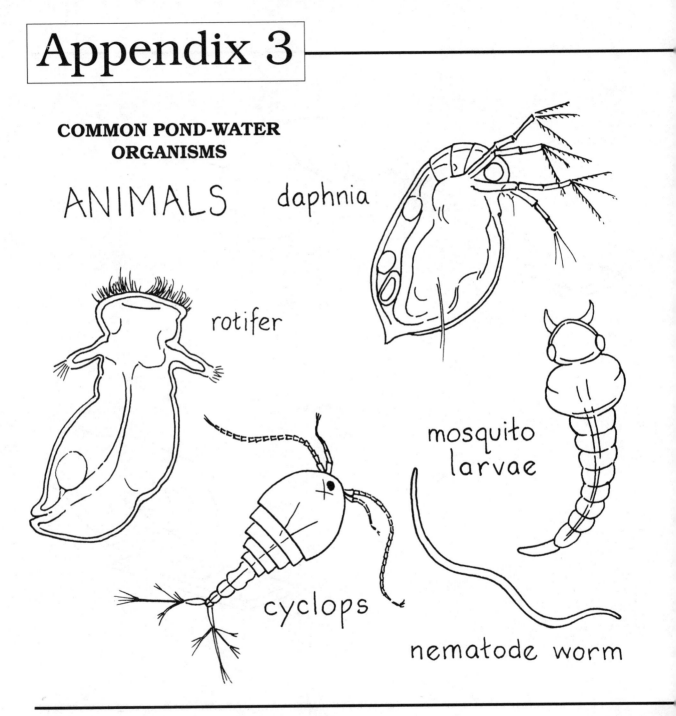

daphnia

rotifer

mosquito larvae

cyclops

nematode worm

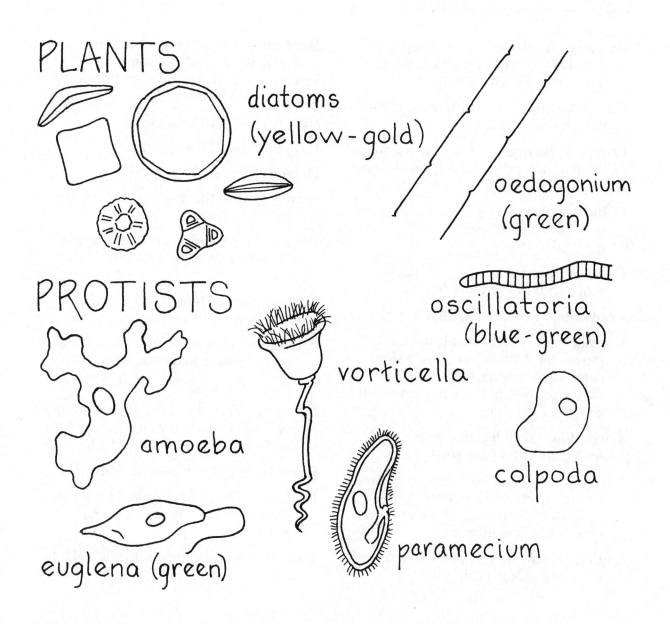

PLANTS

diatoms
(yellow-gold)

oedogonium
(green)

PROTISTS

oscillatoria
(blue-green)

vorticella

amoeba

colpoda

euglena (green)

paramecium

Glossary

Catalyst A substance that changes the speed of a chemical reaction, but is not changed itself.

Circumference The distance around the outside of a circle.

Coarse adjustment Raises and lowers the microscope lenses large distances from the object being viewed.

Cohesive force The attraction between molecules of the same material.

Compound microscope A microscope with two or more lenses.

Converge To come together at a point.

Convex lens A lens that is thicker in the center than on its edges; a single convex lens curves outward on one side; a double convex lens curves outward on both sides.

Cotyledon Seed leaf that stores food for a plant embryo of seed plants.

Crustacean A water-breathing animal having two sets of antennae, jointed bodies and limbs, and commonly covered with a crustlike shell.

Cuticle Dead skin around the base and sides of the fingernail.

Daphnia A small type of crustacean that is often called a "water flea" because it appears to jump through its watery environment.

Decompose To break apart.

Dehydrating Losing water.

Dermis Inner layer of skin.

Dicot A plant that has two cotyledons. Beans are dicots.

Dormancy period A time of inactivity; organisms do not grow during this time.

Double convex lens A convex lens that curves outward on both sides.

Emulsion A suspension of two liquids; some separate upon standing.

Enzyme Catalysts found in living cells.

Epicotyl The part of the embryo (baby plant inside a seed) that develops into the first true leaves of the plant.

Epidermis Outer layer of skin.

Erosion The loosening, and eventual wearing away, of particles that make up an object.

Evaporates Changes from a liquid into a gas.

Expand   To get larger.

Eyepiece   The microscope lens closest to your eye.

Field of vision   The area viewed through a microscope.

Fingerprint   Pattern formed by the ridges on the tips of a finger.

Focal length   The distance from the focal point to the lens.

Focal point   The place where converging light rays meet.

Focus   To produce a sharp, clear image.

Germination   The beginning of growth or development of an embryo (baby plant) inside a seed.

Hypha   Any of the threadlike parts that make up the mycelium of a fungus.

Hypocotyl   The part of the embryo (baby plant inside a seed) that develops into the stem of the plant.

Immiscible   Liquids that do not mix together.

Latex   Sap from rubber trees.

Lunula   Whitish, half-moon area on the fingernails; found next to the cuticles; all growth of the nail takes place beneath this area.

Magnification   The enlargement of an object's image.

Magnify   To cause to appear larger.

Melanin   A pigment that determines color of hair, skin, and other animal tissues.

Monocot   Seed with one cotyledon.

Mycelium   The tangled mass of hypha parts in a fungus.

Nail bed   Area beneath the fingernail; blood in this area gives the nail its pink color.

Nitrogen-fixing bacteria   Bacteria that change nitrogen gas into usable nitrogen compounds for plant use.

Objective lens   The microscope lens closest to the object being viewed.

Opaque   Cannot be seen through.

Penicillium   A bluish-green mold used to make the antibiotic penicillin. It is also used in making cheeses such as Roquefort.

Phloem   Plant tubes that carry dissolved food substances.

Pupil   The opening in the eye that shrinks or expands in response to light.

Radicle   Part of the embryo (baby plant inside seed) that develops into the main root of the plant.

Refract   To change direction; light traveling in one direction can be refracted (bent) so that its direction is changed.

Retina   A special screen on the back inside wall of the eye; light rays converge here to form images.

Root   Area beneath the lunula on a fingernail.

Sap   A liquid mixture of water, sugars, and minerals found in plants.

Single convex lens   A convex lens that curves outward on one side.

Symbiosis   When two organisms, living together, are mutually benefited.

Transparent   Can be seen through clearly.

Viscosity   The property that causes a liquid not to flow easily; its thickness.

Wet mount   A slide specimen that has been prepared with a drop of water and covered with a small piece of glass.

Xylem   Water-carrying tubes in plants.

Index

water:
> transportation in plants, 44–47
> vessels in plants, 46, 47, 59

water fleas, 72–75

xylem, 46, 47, 59
> definition of, 46
> location of, 59